The Betfair Market Is Basically Giving You The Money

Introduction

I decided on the book title for the obvious reason that the Betfair UK and Irish horse racing markets will offer you the money but only if you know where to look!

Now most punters or traders cannot see this as they follow the hype being pumped out on social media and racing channels.

These money making opportunities on a typical days horse racing in the UK and Irish Betfair markets occur no more than ten times per day. I have spent a great deal of time analysing these markets recording and analysing data and then building profitable Betfair trading strategies around this.

Are these Betfair trading strategies difficult?

No they are not but they are profitable if you execute them correctly. In fact these Betfair trading strategies can be automated and that is where the beauty lies in these strategies. These strategies work equally as well when applied manually.

A typical day's trading using the main strategy outlined in this book was as follows,

5 trades
4 won
1 lost

For £10 stake profit was £130.

I had this main Betfair trading strategy running on auto pilot (automated) drinking Barbados Banks beer in the garden at home (UK) people who know me know I love Barbados.

Another day's trading produced the following results,

8 trades
3 won
5 lost

For £10 stake profit was £75.

Now do not get me wrong you will have losing days that is inevitable but we are looking for long term profit over a month and over the years.

We will now move onto outlining this main excellent Betfair horse trading strategy.

Some Traders Make It Complicated

I have over 25 years I.T. experience working on software development and relational databases, and I have modelled and implemented many Betfair trading bots to automate different trading strategies. Some of these strategies were quite complex but I have found that a simple strategy for a given Betfair market works the best. Once you have found your market and an entry and exit position to that market then automating this trading strategy is quite easy with the right tools. I use the excellent trading software tool Bet Angel to implement and automate my trading strategies. Now you can trade manually just by using the Betfair screen. The main trading strategy described in this book can be automated or used manually the choice is yours.

Why I Do Not Like Trading Pre-Off

Basically I do not like spending hours in front of a computer and yes you could automate the pre-off trading but I find when trading large amounts of money through Betfair I want to be there watching the markets. You could rely on stop losses to reduce your liabilities but that is easier said than done as finding the right time to fire a stop loss is difficult. You can sometimes fire the stop loss too early trading out for a red position too often. The same applies to greening up too early and losing potential profits. Now do not get me wrong you can make a significant daily profit by manually trading Betfair horse racing markets pre-off i.e. before a race starts. Some traders do automate trading pre-off but one trading strategy does not fit all Betfair markets. A generic strategy across all markets tends not to work as each market does not exhibit the same characteristics. Some markets have low liquidity or are tight handicap races the list is endless. The trading strategy described in this book is in-play and you can profit significantly using small stakes.

Summary Of How The In-Play Trading Strategy Works

This main Betfair trading strategy is only interested in UK and Irish horse racing markets which exhibit certain characteristics which we will discuss later. Now this will only trade a few races per day and this is intentional as we want to make our money and not expose ourselves to unnecessary risk. We want to trade a small number of races with consistent profits. Now you will get losing days but that is to be expected.

I have also added a bonus large priced Betfair trading strategy which is optional. You can run both strategies outlined in this book in parallel with no conflict. I have also added a tailoring option to the main Betfair trading strategy outlined in this book.

Betfair Market Odds Movements

This is an important subject and you must fully understand this to make the most out of this main Betfair trading strategy.

I am talking about Betfair market odds movements starting from 10 minutes before a race starts up to 10 seconds before the race starts. This 10 minute window is the key to this main Betfair trading strategy and I will explain.

If we look at the table below you will see some examples of Betfair odds movements from 10 minutes before the race starts up to 10 seconds before the race starts.

So what can we learn from this information?

Fav Position	10 Minute Odds	10 Seconds Odds	Odds Difference
2	5.20	3.55	1.65
3	4.9	3.7	1.2
2	6.4	5.1	1.3
2	6	4.7	1.3
2	5.4	4	1.4
3	6	4.7	1.3
1	5.2	3.85	1.35
2	5.7	4.4	1.3
3	6.6	4.5	2.1
3	5.5	4.4	1.1
3	13	11.5	1.5
3	6.2	4.7	1.5
3	6.8	4.6	2.2

The Main Betfair Trading Strategy Explained

1. This main Betfair trading strategy revolves around the top 3 in the betting and is fixed 10 minutes before the race starts. These top 3 in the betting remain fixed throughout the race pre-off and in-play!

2. We are only interested in the horses highlighted in **(1)** above if their decimal odds range is greater than or equal to **2.0** and less than equal to **7.0** approximately 5 seconds before the race starts then we place a trade on our selection(s).

3. Using the top 3 horses in the betting identified in (1) above the decimal odds differential from 10 minutes before the race starts and 10 seconds before the race starts must be greater than or equal to 1.2. **This decimal odds differential is calculated approximately 5 seconds before the race starts!**

   This is a hard rule that must not be broken!

- *Once the top 3 in the betting are identified 10 minutes before the race starts we use these top 3 favourites throughout the process even if any of them moves out of the top 3 in the betting during this 10 minute window.*

We only place a trade/bet on selection(s) when the selection meets the above 3 conditions!

Now you can place bet/trade 5 seconds before race off or in-play it is up to you!

Now this is a simple Betfair trading strategy but it works and it makes money on a daily basis!

I will now show you a typical day's racing and we will use the **20th September 2023** as a real example of making money.

Please make sure you understand this main Betfair trading strategy before moving forward!

A Typical Days Trading

20th September 2023 Betfair Trading Day

I was using £2 trading stakes to make it simple but this scales easily.

8 trades
3 won
5 lost

Total outlay £16

Lost trades £10

Won trades £15.66

Profit (without commission) **£5.66**

If we had used **£10** trading stake our profit would have been **£28.30**.

Let us look at these 3 winning trades in more detail.

Beverley 2.20 Winner Rogue Enforcer

Decimal odds difference 10 minutes and 10 seconds before the race starts **1.2** (calculated 5 seconds before the race starts).

I was only using £2 stakes for examples in this book but just simply multiply by 5 as if you were using a £10 stake.

Our stake of £2 produces a profit of **£5.50**.

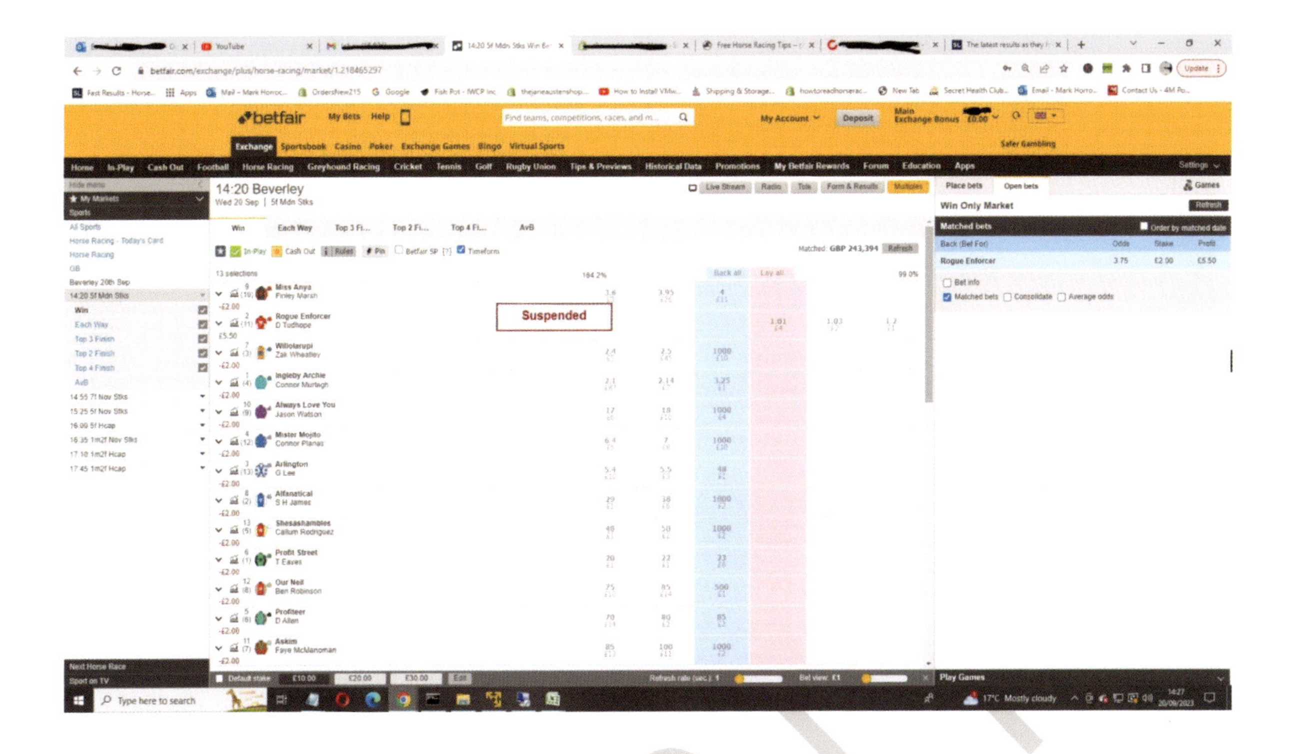

Decimal Odds 10 Minutes Before The Race Starts

9/20/2023 14:10:00: Miss Anya: Back Fav1 Price 10 Mins = 4.4
9/20/2023 14:10:00: Rogue Enforcer: Back Fav2 Price 10 Mins = 5.2
9/20/2023 14:10:00: Willolarupi: Back Fav3 Price 10 Mins = 5.8

Decimal Odds 10 Seconds Before The Race Starts

9/20/2023 14:19:50: Miss Anya: Back Fav1 Price 10 Secs = 4.3
9/20/2023 14:19:50: Rogue Enforcer: Back Fav2 Price 10 Secs = 4
9/20/2023 14:19:50: Willolarupi: Back Fav3 Price 10 Secs = 7.8

Decimal Odds Difference 10 Minutes And 10 Seconds Before The Race Starts

9/20/2023 14:19:55: Miss Anya: Diff Back Fav1 Price = 4.4 - 4.3 = 0.1
9/20/2023 14:19:55: Rogue Enforcer: Diff Back Fav2 Price = 5.2 - 4 = 1.2
9/20/2023 14:19:55: Willolarupi: Diff Back Fav3 Price = 5.8 - 7.8 = -2

You will notice the green line above and the decimal odds difference in red as **1.2**.

The decimal odds of the horse Rogue Enforcer was **5.2** approximately 10 minutes before the race started.

The decimal odds of the horse Rogue Enforcer was **4** approximately 10 seconds before the race started.

Decimal Odds Difference is 5.2 – 4 = 1.2

Our horse Rogue Enforcer won the race 11/4.

I got decimal odds of **3.75** for a profit of **£5.50** for a **£2** stake.

This was a valid selection as it passed the conditions of this main Betfair trading strategy,

Decimal odds differential was greater than or equal to 1.2 approximately 5 seconds before the race started.

The decimal odds of our selection Rogue Enforcer was between 2.0 and 7.0 approximately 5 seconds before the race started.

Now I will not repeat these Betfair trading strategy conditions above for every race example as it would become tedious.

Kelso 5.15 Winner Darkest Day

Decimal odds difference 10 minutes and 10 seconds before the race starts **1.2** (calculated 5 seconds before the race starts).

I was only using £2 stakes for examples in this book but just simply multiply by 5 as if you were using a £10 stake.

Our stake of £2 produces a profit of **£5.06**.

Decimal Odds 10 Minutes Before The Race Starts

9/20/2023 17:05:00: Zamond: Back Fav1 Price 10 Mins = 4

9/20/2023 17:05:00: Ten Ten Twenty: Back Fav2 Price 10 Mins = 4

9/20/2023 17:05:00: Darkest Day: Back Fav3 Price 10 Mins = 5.3

Decimal Odds 10 Seconds Before The Race Starts

9/20/2023 17:14:50: Zamond: Back Fav1 Price 10 Secs = 3.7
9/20/2023 17:14:50: Ten Ten Twenty: Back Fav2 Price 10 Secs = 4.5
9/20/2023 17:14:50: Darkest Day: Back Fav3 Price 10 Secs = 4.1

Decimal Odds Difference 10 Minutes And 10 Seconds Before The Race Starts

9/20/2023 17:14:55: Zamond: Diff Back Fav1 Price = 4 - 3.7 = 0.3
9/20/2023 17:14:55: Ten Ten Twenty: Diff Back Fav2 Price = 4 - 4.5 = -0.5
9/20/2023 17:14:55: Darkest Day: Diff Back Fav3 Price = 5.3 - 4.1 = 1.2

Decimal Odds Difference is 5.3 – 4.1 = 1.2

Our horse Darkest Day won the race 11/4.

I got decimal odds of **3.53** for a profit of **£5.06** for a **£2** stake.

Listowel 2.45 Winner The Wallpark

Decimal odds difference 10 minutes and 10 seconds before the race starts **1.25** (calculated 5 seconds before the race starts).

I was only using £2 stakes for examples in this book but just simply multiply by 5 as if you were using a £10 stake.

Our stake of £2 produces a profit of **£5.10**.

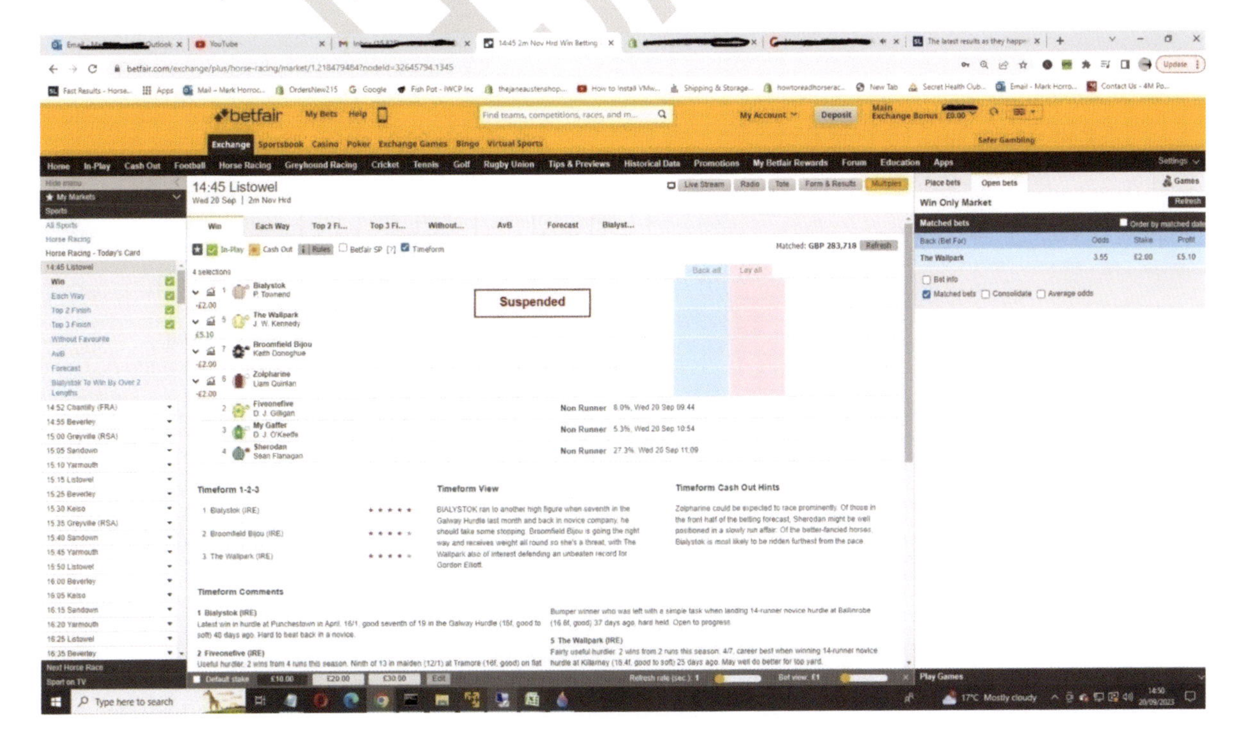

Decimal Odds 10 Minutes Before The Race Starts

9/20/2023 14:35:00: Bialystok: Back Fav1 Price 10 Mins = 1.6
9/20/2023 14:35:00: The Wallpark: Back Fav2 Price 10 Mins = 5
9/20/2023 14:35:00: Broomfield Bijou: Back Fav3 Price 10 Mins = 7

Decimal Odds 10 Seconds Before The Race Starts

9/20/2023 14:44:50: Bialystok: Back Fav1 Price 10 Secs = 1.79
9/20/2023 14:44:50: The Wallpark: Back Fav2 Price 10 Secs = 3.75
9/20/2023 14:44:50: Broomfield Bijou: Back Fav3 Price 10 Secs = 6.4

Decimal Odds Difference 10 Minutes And 10 Seconds Before The Race Starts

9/20/2023 14:44:55: Bialystok: Diff Back Fav1 Price = 1.6 - 1.79 = -0.19
9/20/2023 14:44:55: The Wallpark: Diff Back Fav2 Price = 5 - 3.75 = 1.25
9/20/2023 14:44:55: Broomfield Bijou: Diff Back Fav3 Price = 7 - 6.4 = 0.6

Decimal Odds Difference is 5 – 3.75 = 1.25

Our horse The Wallpark won the race 5/2.

I got decimal odds of **3.55** for a profit of **£5.10** for a **£2** stake.

We will now look at other example days trading.

Other Examples

23rd September 2023 Betfair Trading Day

Listowel 1.35 Winner Smooth Tom

Decimal odds difference 10 minutes and 10 seconds before the race starts **2.05** (calculated 5 seconds before the race starts).

I was only using £2 stakes for examples in this book but just simply multiply by 5 as if you were using a £10 stake.

Our stake of £2 produces a profit of **£5.83**.

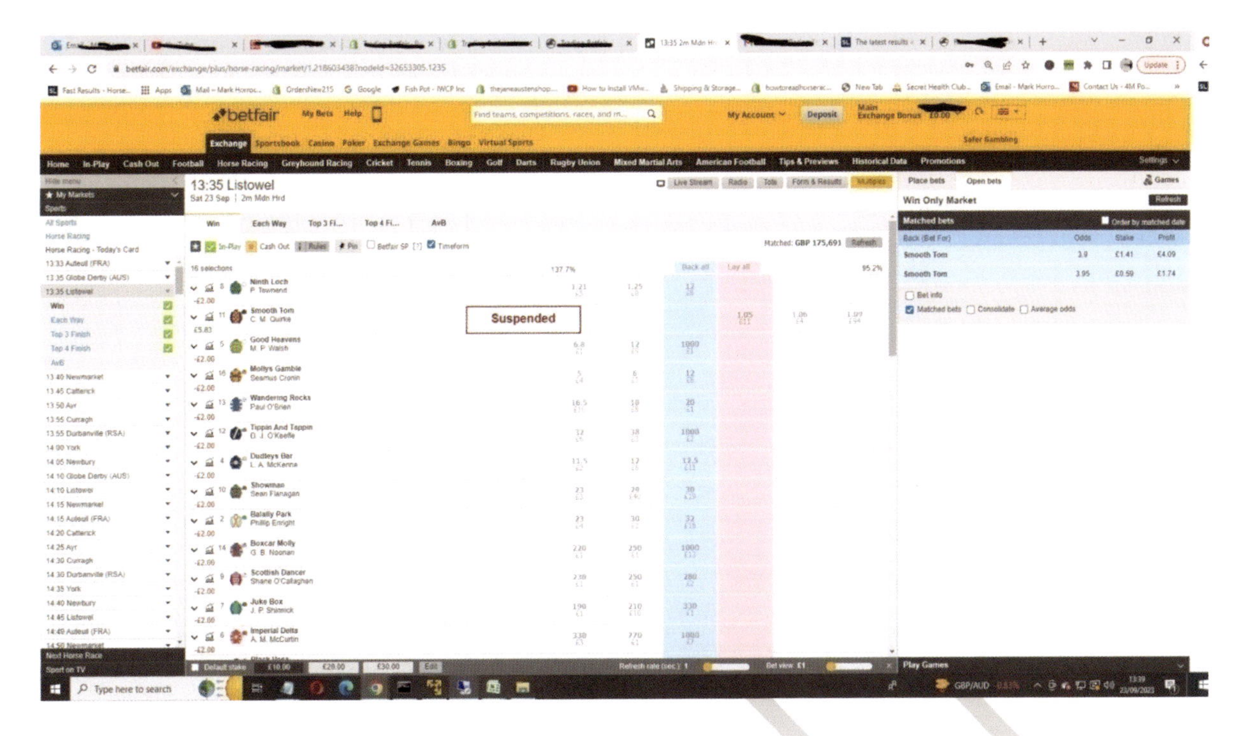

Decimal Odds 10 Minutes Before The Race Starts

9/23/2023 13:25:00: Ninth Loch: Back Fav1 Price 10 Mins = 2.06
9/23/2023 13:25:00: Good Heavens: Back Fav2 Price 10 Mins = 5.2
9/23/2023 13:25:00: Smooth Tom: Back Fav3 Price 10 Mins = 6

Decimal Odds 10 Seconds Before The Race Starts

9/23/2023 13:34:50: Ninth Loch: Back Fav1 Price 10 Secs = 2.48
9/23/2023 13:34:50: Good Heavens: Back Fav2 Price 10 Secs = 4.9
9/23/2023 13:34:50: Smooth Tom: Back Fav3 Price 10 Secs = 3.95

Decimal Odds Difference 10 Minutes And 10 Seconds Before The Race Starts

9/23/2023 13:34:55: Ninth Loch: Diff Back Fav1 Price = 2.06 - 2.48 = -0.42
9/23/2023 13:34:55: Good Heavens: Diff Back Fav2 Price = 5.2 - 4.9 = 0.3
9/23/2023 13:34:55: Smooth Tom: Diff Back Fav3 Price = 6 - 3.95 = 2.05

Decimal Odds Difference is 6 – 3.95 = 2.05

Our horse Smooth Tom won the race 5/2.

I got decimal odds of **3.90** for a profit of **£5.83** for a **£2** stake.

York 4.20 Winner Vintage Clarets

Decimal odds difference 10 minutes and 10 seconds before the race starts **1.6** (calculated 5 seconds before the race starts).

I was only using £2 stakes for examples in this book but just simply multiply by 5 as if you were using a £10 stake.

Our stake of £2 produces a profit of **£12.80**.

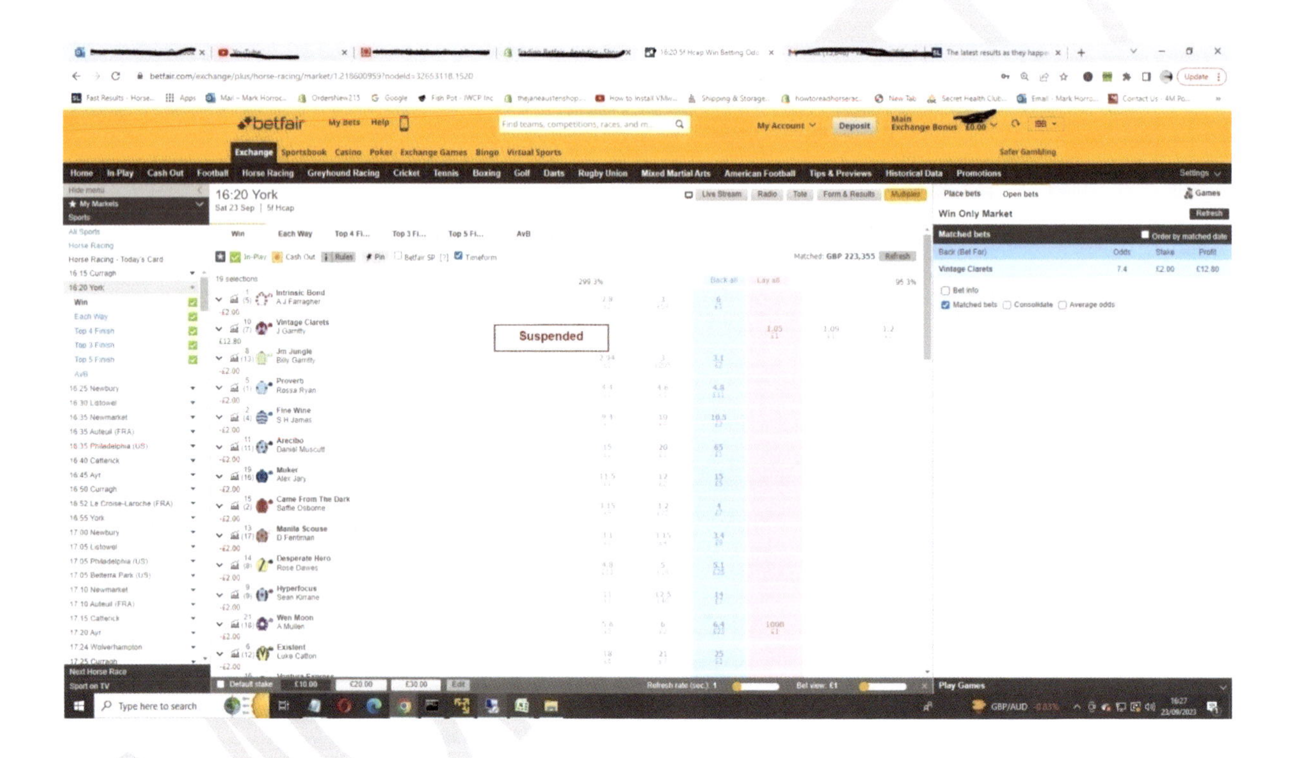

Decimal Odds 10 Minutes Before The Race Starts

9/23/2023 16:10:00: Intrinsic Bond: Back Fav1 Price 10 Mins = 6
9/23/2023 16:10:00: Vintage Clarets: Back Fav2 Price 10 Mins = 8.6
9/23/2023 16:10:00: Jm Jungle: Back Fav3 Price 10 Mins = 9.2

Decimal Odds 10 Seconds Before The Race Starts

9/23/2023 16:19:50: Intrinsic Bond: Back Fav1 Price 10 Secs = 4.9
9/23/2023 16:19:50: Vintage Clarets: Back Fav2 Price 10 Secs = 7
9/23/2023 16:19:50: Jm Jungle: Back Fav3 Price 10 Secs = 10

Decimal Odds Difference 10 Minutes And 10 Seconds Before The Race Starts

9/23/2023 16:19:55: Intrinsic Bond: Diff Back Fav1 Price = 6 - 4.9 = 1.1
9/23/2023 16:19:55: Vintage Clarets: Diff Back Fav2 Price = 8.6 - 7 = 1.6
9/23/2023 16:19:55: Jm Jungle: Diff Back Fav3 Price = 9.2 - 10 = -0.8

Decimal Odds Difference is 8.6 – 7.0 = 1.6

Our horse Vintage Clarets won the race 5/1.

I got decimal odds of **7.4** for a profit of **£12.80** for a **£2** stake.

You will notice this selection was just on the outer limit of the decimal odds range condition 2.0 to 7.0 for this Betfair trading strategy and I actually matched at decimal odds of 7.4 when the order entered the market.

24th September 2023 Betfair Trading Day

Hamilton 5.10 Winner Lunacy

Decimal odds difference 10 minutes and 10 seconds before the race starts **1.3** (calculated 5 seconds before the race starts).

I was only using £2 stakes for examples in this book but just simply multiply by 5 as if you were using a £10 stake.

Our stake of £2 produces a profit of **£8.00**.

Decimal Odds 10 Minutes Before The Race Starts

9/24/2023 17:00:00: Barrolo: Back Fav1 Price 10 Mins = 2.78
9/24/2023 17:00:00: Blue Antares: Back Fav2 Price 10 Mins = 5.3
9/24/2023 17:00:00: Lunacy: Back Fav3 Price 10 Mins = 5.8

Decimal Odds 10 Seconds Before The Race Starts

9/24/2023 17:09:50: Barrolo: Back Fav1 Price 10 Secs = 3.3
9/24/2023 17:09:50: Blue Antares: Back Fav2 Price 10 Secs = 4.6
9/24/2023 17:09:50: Lunacy: Back Fav3 Price 10 Secs = 4.5

Decimal Odds Difference 10 Minutes And 10 Seconds Before The Race Starts

9/24/2023 17:09:55: Barrolo: Diff Back Fav1 Price = 2.78 - 3.3 = -0.52
9/24/2023 17:09:55: Blue Antares: Diff Back Fav2 Price = 5.3 - 4.6 = 0.7
9/24/2023 17:09:55: Lunacy: Diff Back Fav3 Price = 5.8 - 4.5 = 1.3

Decimal Odds Difference is 5.8 – 4.5 = 1.3

Our horse Lunacy won the race 3/1.

I got decimal odds of **5.0** for a profit of **£8** for a **£2** stake.

25th September 2023 Betfair Trading Day

Down Royal 4.45 Winner Red Trail

Decimal odds difference 10 minutes and 10 seconds before the race starts **1.6** (calculated 5 seconds before the race starts).

I was only using £2 stakes for examples in this book but just simply multiply by 5 as if you were using a £10 stake.

Our stake of £2 produces a profit of **£7.62**.

Decimal Odds 10 Minutes Before The Race Starts

9/25/2023 16:35:00: Mr Mills: Back Fav1 Price 10 Mins = 5.2
9/25/2023 16:35:00: Red Trail: Back Fav2 Price 10 Mins = 7
9/25/2023 16:35:00: Lisamaria: Back Fav3 Price 10 Mins = 7.2

Decimal Odds 10 Seconds Before The Race Starts

9/25/2023 16:44:50: Mr Mills: Back Fav1 Price 10 Secs = 5.8
9/25/2023 16:44:50: Red Trail: Back Fav2 Price 10 Secs = 5.4
9/25/2023 16:44:50: Lisamaria: Back Fav3 Price 10 Secs = 10.5

Decimal Odds Difference 10 Minutes And 10 Seconds Before The Race Starts

9/25/2023 16:44:55: Mr Mills: Diff Back Fav1 Price = 5.2 - 5.8 = -0.6
9/25/2023 16:44:55: Red Trail: Diff Back Fav2 Price = 7 - 5.4 = 1.6
9/25/2023 16:44:55: Lisamaria: Diff Back Fav3 Price = 7.2 - 10.5 = -3.3

Decimal Odds Difference is 7.0 – 5.4 = 1.6

Our horse Red Trail won the race 4/1.

I got decimal odds of **4.81** for a profit of **£7.62** for a **£2** stake.

Warwick 3.05 Winner Are U Wise To That

Decimal odds difference 10 minutes and 10 seconds before the race starts **1.2** (calculated 5 seconds before the race starts).

I was only using £2 stakes for examples in this book but just simply multiply by 5 as if you were using a £10 stake.

Our stake of £2 produces a profit of **£11.60**.

Decimal Odds 10 Minutes Before The Race Starts

9/25/2023 14:55:00: Notnowlinda: Back Fav1 Price 10 Mins = 3
9/25/2023 14:55:00: Are U Wise To That: Back Fav2 Price 10 Mins = 7
9/25/2023 14:55:00: Gold Link: Back Fav3 Price 10 Mins = 7.6

Decimal Odds 10 Seconds Before The Race Starts

9/25/2023 15:04:50: Notnowlinda: Back Fav1 Price 10 Secs = 3.7
9/25/2023 15:04:50: Are U Wise To That: Back Fav2 Price 10 Secs = 5.8

9/25/2023 15:04:50: Gold Link: Back Fav3 Price 10 Secs = 7.6

Decimal Odds Difference 10 Minutes And 10 Seconds Before The Race Starts

9/25/2023 15:04:55: Notnowlinda: Diff Back Fav1 Price = 3 - 3.7 = -0.7
9/25/2023 15:04:55: Are U Wise To That: Diff Back Fav2 Price = 7 - 5.8 = 1.2
9/25/2023 15:04:55: Gold Link: Diff Back Fav3 Price = 7.6 - 7.6 = 0

Decimal Odds Difference is 7.0 – 5.8 = 1.2

Our horse Are U Wise To That won the race 4/1.

I got decimal odds of **6.8** for a profit of **£11.60** for a **£2** stake.

Leicester 2.05 Winner Ceilidh

Decimal odds difference 10 minutes and 10 seconds before the race starts **1.3** (calculated 5 seconds before the race starts).

I was only using £2 stakes for examples in this book but just simply multiply by 5 as if you were using a £10 stake.

Our stake of £2 produces a profit of **£10**.

Decimal Odds 10 Minutes Before The Race Starts

9/25/2023 13:55:00: Ratafia: Back Fav1 Price 10 Mins = 5
9/25/2023 13:55:00: Diamondsinthesand: Back Fav2 Price 10 Mins = 6.8
9/25/2023 13:55:00: Ceilidh: Back Fav3 Price 10 Mins = 7

Decimal Odds 10 Seconds Before The Race Starts

9/25/2023 14:04:50: Ratafia: Back Fav1 Price 10 Secs = 4.8
9/25/2023 14:04:50: Diamondsinthesand: Back Fav2 Price 10 Secs = 6.2
9/25/2023 14:04:50: Ceilidh: Back Fav3 Price 10 Secs = 5.7

Decimal Odds Difference 10 Minutes And 10 Seconds Before The Race Starts

9/25/2023 14:04:55: Ratafia: Diff Back Fav1 Price = 5 - 4.8 = 0.2

9/25/2023 14:04:55: Diamondsinthesand: Diff Back Fav2 Price = 6.8 - 6.2 = 0.6
9/25/2023 14:04:55: Ceilidh: Diff Back Fav3 Price = 7 - 5.7 = 1.3

Decimal Odds Difference is 7.0 – 5.7 = 1.3

Our horse Ceilidh won the race 4/1.

I got decimal odds of **6.0** for a profit of **£10.00** for a **£2** stake.

26th September 2023 Betfair Trading Day

Newcastle 4.55 Winner Seahorse Syd

Decimal odds difference 10 minutes and 10 seconds before the race starts **1.4** (calculated 5 seconds before the race starts).

I actually increased my stake from £2 to £3 as an example for this book and to show scaling this trading strategy.

Our stake of £3 produces a profit of **£16.79**.

Decimal Odds 10 Minutes Before The Race Starts

9/26/2023 16:45:00: Due Consideration: Back Fav1 Price 10 Mins = 2.56
9/26/2023 16:45:00: Surging Tide: Back Fav2 Price 10 Mins = 3.05
9/26/2023 16:45:00: Seahorse Syd: Back Fav3 Price 10 Mins = 7.4

Decimal Odds 10 Seconds Before The Race Starts

9/26/2023 16:54:50: Due Consideration: Back Fav1 Price 10 Secs = 3.3
9/26/2023 16:54:50: Surging Tide: Back Fav2 Price 10 Secs = 2.52
9/26/2023 16:54:50: Seahorse Syd: Back Fav3 Price 10 Secs = 6

Decimal Odds Difference 10 Minutes And 10 Seconds Before The Race Starts

9/26/2023 16:54:55: Due Consideration: Diff Back Fav1 Price = 2.56 - 3.3 = -0.74
9/26/2023 16:54:55: Surging Tide: Diff Back Fav2 Price = 3.05 - 2.52 = 0.53
9/26/2023 16:54:55: Seahorse Syd: Diff Back Fav3 Price = 7.4 - 6 = 1.4

Decimal Odds Difference is 7.4 – 6.0= 1.4

Our horse Seahorse Syd won the race 9/2.

I got decimal odds of **6.60** for a profit of **£16.79** for a **£3** stake.

Nottingham 2.05 Winner Irish Nectar

Decimal odds difference 10 minutes and 10 seconds before the race starts **1.8** (calculated 5 seconds before the race starts).

I actually increased my stake from £2 to £3 as an example for this book and to show scaling this trading strategy.

Our stake of £3 produces a profit of **£20.32**.

Decimal Odds 10 Minutes Before The Race Starts

9/26/2023 13:55:00: Mashadi: Back Fav1 Price 10 Mins = 3.3
9/26/2023 13:55:00: Jungle Jim: Back Fav2 Price 10 Mins = 5.7
9/26/2023 13:55:00: Irish Nectar: Back Fav3 Price 10 Mins = 6.6

Decimal Odds 10 Seconds Before The Race Starts

9/26/2023 14:04:50: Mashadi: Back Fav1 Price 10 Secs = 3.6
9/26/2023 14:04:50: Jungle Jim: Back Fav2 Price 10 Secs = 6
9/26/2023 14:04:50: Irish Nectar: Back Fav3 Price 10 Secs = 4.8

Decimal Odds Difference 10 Minutes And 10 Seconds Before The Race Starts

9/26/2023 14:04:55: Mashadi: Diff Back Fav1 Price = 3.3 - 3.6 = -0.3
9/26/2023 14:04:55: Jungle Jim: Diff Back Fav2 Price = 5.7 - 6 = -0.3
9/26/2023 14:04:55: Irish Nectar: Diff Back Fav3 Price = 6.6 - 4.8 = 1.8

Decimal Odds Difference is 6.6 – 4.8= 1.8

Our horse Irish Nectar won the race 100/30.

I got decimal odds of **7.78** for a profit of **£20.32** for a **£3** stake.

27th September 2023 Betfair Trading Day

Kempton 8-00 Winner Embarked

Decimal odds difference 10 minutes and 10 seconds before the race starts **1.2** (calculated 5 seconds before the race starts).

I actually lowered my stake from £3 to £1 as an example for this book and to show scaling back this trading strategy.

Our stake of £1 produces a profit of **£5.00.**

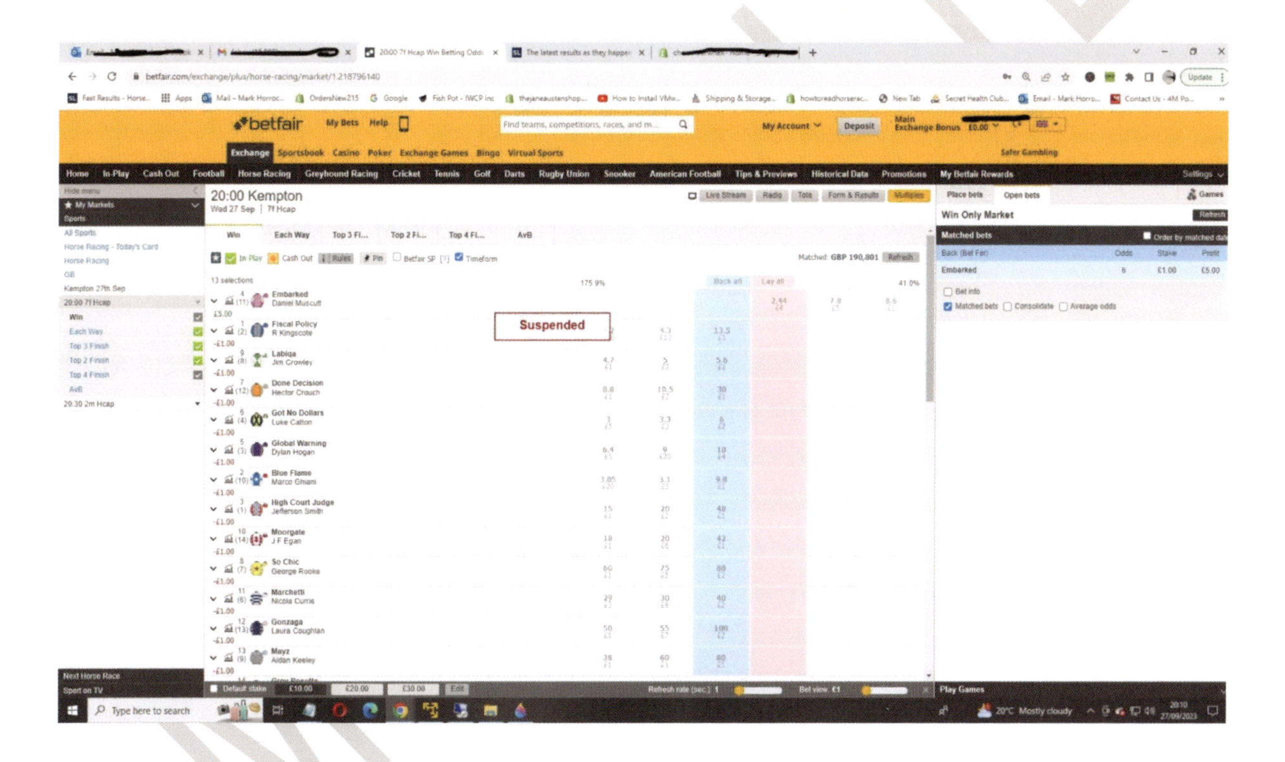

Decimal Odds 10 Minutes Before The Race Starts

9/27/2023 19:50:00: Fiscal Policy: Back Fav1 Price 10 Mins = 4.4
9/27/2023 19:50:00: Embarked: Back Fav2 Price 10 Mins = 5.1
9/27/2023 19:50:00: Labiqa: Back Fav3 Price 10 Mins = 6.6

Decimal Odds 10 Seconds Before The Race Starts

9/27/2023 19:59:50: Fiscal Policy: Back Fav1 Price 10 Secs = 4.6

9/27/2023 19:59:50: Embarked: Back Fav2 Price 10 Secs = 3.9
9/27/2023 19:59:50: Labiqa: Back Fav3 Price 10 Secs = 9

Decimal Odds Difference 10 Minutes And 10 Seconds Before The Race Starts

9/27/2023 19:59:55: Fiscal Policy: Diff Back Fav1 Price = 4.4 - 4.6 = -0.2
9/27/2023 19:59:55: Embarked: Diff Back Fav2 Price = 5.1 - 3.9 = 1.2
9/27/2023 19:59:55: Labiqa: Diff Back Fav3 Price = 6.6 - 9 = -2.4

Decimal Odds Difference is 5.1 – 3.9= 1.2

Our horse Embarked won the race 3/1.

I got decimal odds of **6.00** for a profit of **£5.00** for a **£1** stake.

Redcar 4.25 Winner Pillar Of Hope

Decimal odds difference 10 minutes and 10 seconds before the race starts **1.8** (calculated 5 seconds before the race starts).

I actually lowered my stake from £3 to £1 as an example for this book and to show scaling back this trading strategy.

Our stake of £1 produces a profit of **£4.20**.

Decimal Odds 10 Minutes Before The Race Starts

9/27/2023 16:15:00: Casilli: Back Fav1 Price 10 Mins = 6.8
9/27/2023 16:15:00: Blueflagflyinghigh: Back Fav2 Price 10 Mins = 7.2
9/27/2023 16:15:00: Pillar Of Hope: Back Fav3 Price 10 Mins = 7.8

Decimal Odds 10 Seconds Before The Race Starts

9/27/2023 16:24:50: Casilli: Back Fav1 Price 10 Secs = 7.4
9/27/2023 16:24:50: Blueflagflyinghigh: Back Fav2 Price 10 Secs = 8.6
9/27/2023 16:24:50: Pillar Of Hope: Back Fav3 Price 10 Secs = 6

Decimal Odds Difference 10 Minutes And 10 Seconds Before The Race Starts

9/27/2023 16:24:55: Casilli: Diff Back Fav1 Price = 6.8 - 7.4 = -0.6
9/27/2023 16:24:55: Blueflagflyinghigh: Diff Back Fav2 Price = 7.2 - 8.6 = -1.4

9/27/2023 16:24:55: Pillar Of Hope: Diff Back Fav3 Price = 7.8 - 6 = 1.8

Decimal Odds Difference is 7.8– 6.0= 1.8

Our horse Pillar Of Hope won the race 9/2F.

I got decimal odds of **5.20** for a profit of **£4.20** for a **£1** stake.

Perth 3.30 Winner Thunder In Milan

Decimal odds difference 10 minutes and 10 seconds before the race starts **1.2** (calculated 5 seconds before the race starts).

I actually lowered my stake from £3 to £1 as an example for this book and to show scaling back this trading strategy.

Our stake of £1 produces a profit of **£4.00**.

Decimal Odds 10 Minutes Before The Race Starts

9/27/2023 15:20:00: Sputnik: Back Fav1 Price 10 Mins = 5.1
9/27/2023 15:20:00: A Place Apart: Back Fav2 Price 10 Mins = 5.8
9/27/2023 15:20:00: Thunder In Milan: Back Fav3 Price 10 Mins = 5.9

Decimal Odds 10 Seconds Before The Race Starts

9/27/2023 15:29:50: Sputnik: Back Fav1 Price 10 Secs = 7.2
9/27/2023 15:29:50: A Place Apart: Back Fav2 Price 10 Secs = 5.8
9/27/2023 15:29:50: Thunder In Milan: Back Fav3 Price 10 Secs = 4.7

Decimal Odds Difference 10 Minutes And 10 Seconds Before The Race Starts

9/27/2023 15:29:55: Sputnik: Diff Back Fav1 Price = 5.1 - 7.2 = -2.1
9/27/2023 15:29:55: A Place Apart: Diff Back Fav2 Price = 5.8 - 5.8 = 0
9/27/2023 15:29:55: Thunder In Milan: Diff Back Fav3 Price = 5.9 - 4.7 = 1.2

Decimal Odds Difference is 5.9 – 4.7 = 1.2

Our horse Thunder In Milan won the race 3/1F.

I got decimal odds of **5.00** for a profit of **£4.00** for a **£1** stake.

Tailoring This Strategy

We can tailor this main Betfair horse racing trading strategy in a number of ways to extract more profit from the market but this is entirely up to you. We adopt the same strategy for this main current Betfair trading system I have outlined earlier in this book but we place an extra trade at larger decimal odds on the selection(s) it has identified. Now you could pick a decimal odds value that you are comfortable with say **40.0** on this second trade this value is up to you. So we would place a further trade of £1 for example on our selection as identified in the main Betfair trading system outlined above in the book. If the horse gets matched at these decimal odds of 40.0 and wins the race we have a very healthy profit indeed for a £10 stake.

Let us look at an example trade below.

2nd October 2023

Newton Abbot 5.15 Winner Kym Eyre

Decimal odds difference 10 minutes and 10 seconds before the race starts **2.4** (calculated 5 seconds before the race starts).

I actually lowered my stake from £3 to £1 as an example for this book and to show scaling back this trading strategy.

Our stake of £1 produces a profit of **£9.00**.

Decimal Odds 10 Minutes Before The Race Starts

10/2/2023 17:05:00: Lady Berlais: Back Fav1 Price 10 Mins = 1.89
10/2/2023 17:05:00: Caitlins Court: Back Fav2 Price 10 Mins = 7.4
10/2/2023 17:05:00: Kym Eyre: Back Fav3 Price 10 Mins = 8.4

Decimal Odds 10 Seconds Before The Race Starts

10/2/2023 17:14:50: Lady Berlais: Back Fav1 Price 10 Secs = 1.9
10/2/2023 17:14:50: Caitlins Court: Back Fav2 Price 10 Secs = 8.2
10/2/2023 17:14:50: Kym Eyre: Back Fav3 Price 10 Secs = 6

Decimal Odds Difference 10 Minutes And 10 Seconds Before The Race Starts

10/2/2023 17:14:55: Lady Berlais: Diff Back Fav1 Price = 1.89 - 1.9 = -0.01
10/2/2023 17:14:55: Caitlins Court: Diff Back Fav2 Price = 7.4 - 8.2 = -0.8
10/2/2023 17:14:55: Kym Eyre: Diff Back Fav3 Price = 8.4 - 6 = 2.4

Decimal Odds Difference is 8.4 – 6.0 = 2.4

Our horse Kym Eyre won the race 9/2.

I got decimal odds of **5.50** for a profit of **£4.50** for a **£1** stake.

The above is the main Betfair trading strategy selection(s) process outlined in this book, now for the second trade on our selection Kym Eyre at larger decimal odds (of your choosing). I used the decimal odds value of **30.0** and placed an extra £1 trade on this selection.

Now our selection Kym Eyre got matched at decimal odds of **30.0** in-play see my automation in-play log extract below.

I have highlighted in green the decimal odds **30.0** that got matched when the race was in-play. It actually hit decimal odds of **40.0** in-play!

Automation in-play log extract

10/2/2023 17:15:54: £ 1.00 Back bet placed on Kym Eyre at 30.00. 10/2/2023 17:15:55: Kym Eyre: Hit 5.5 = 1

10/2/2023 17:15:55: £ 1.00 Back bet placed on Kym Eyre at 5.5. 10/2/2023 17:15:55: Kym Eyre:

10/2/2023 17:16:12: Kym Eyre: Hit 7.0 = 1

10/2/2023 17:16:19: Kym Eyre: Hit 8.0 = 1

10/2/2023 17:16:20: Kym Eyre: Hit 10.0 = 1

10/2/2023 17:16:20: Kym Eyre: Hit 9.5 = 1

10/2/2023 17:16:20: Kym Eyre: Hit 9.0 = 1

10/2/2023 17:16:20: Kym Eyre: Hit 8.5 = 1

10/2/2023 17:17:26: Kym Eyre: Hit 11.0 = 1

10/2/2023 17:17:43: Kym Eyre: Hit 12.0 = 1

10/2/2023 17:17:44: Kym Eyre: Hit 15.0 = 1

10/2/2023 17:17:44: Kym Eyre: Hit 14.0 = 1

10/2/2023 17:17:44: Kym Eyre: Hit 13.0 = 1

10/2/2023 17:18:35: Kym Eyre: Hit 25.0 = 1

10/2/2023 17:18:37: Kym Eyre: Hit 30.0 = 1

10/2/2023 17:20:00: Kym Eyre: Hit 40.0 = 1

10/2/2023 17:20:16: Kym Eyre: Hit 4.5 = 1

10/2/2023 17:20:18: Kym Eyre: Hit 4.0 = 1

10/2/2023 17:20:18: Kym Eyre: Hit 3.75 = 1

10/2/2023 17:20:18: Kym Eyre: Hit 3.5 = 1

10/2/2023 17:20:18: Kym Eyre: Hit 3.0 = 1

10/2/2023 17:20:18: Kym Eyre: Hit 2.5 = 1

10/2/2023 17:20:24: Kym Eyre: Hit 2.0 = 1

10/2/2023 17:20:24: Kym Eyre: Hit 1.91 = 1

10/2/2023 17:20:24: Kym Eyre: Hit 1.81 = 1

10/2/2023 17:20:31: Kym Eyre: Hit 1.71 = 1

10/2/2023 17:20:31: Kym Eyre: Hit 1.61 = 1

10/2/2023 17:21:15: Kym Eyre: Hit 1.51 = 1

10/2/2023 17:21:15: Kym Eyre: Hit 1.41 = 1

10/2/2023 17:21:15: Kym Eyre: Hit 1.31 = 1

10/2/2023 17:21:16: Kym Eyre: Hit 1.21 = 1

10/2/2023 17:21:23: Kym Eyre: Hit 1.11 = 1

10/2/2023 17:21:24: Kym Eyre: Winner = 1

10/2/2023 17:21:28: The market is suspended

A word of caution here!

By placing an extra trade on our selection(s) at higher decimal odds in anticipation it will get matched in-play and win the race is speculative based on the probability of the decimal odds value you have chosen. Now I will guarantee you that you will get matched at these higher decimal odds if your selection loses. The value of the decimal odds you chose is up to you may I suggest you do not be too greedy!

If you are too greedy you will end up losing more money, it may be better to take a cautious approach with your decimal odds selection we are after long term profits here.

A different approach!

You could take an approach whereby you just place one trade on the selection(s) selected in this main Betfair trading strategy at the higher decimal odds of say 30.0 whilst ignoring the initial lower decimal odds trade you would normally have executed. You then play the waiting game to get matched at decimal odds of 30.0 and win the race and take your profit.

You might have days where this approach does not make a profit but one winning trade at decimal odds of 30.0 is a great deal of profit to play with! I have actually used decimal odds of 100.0 which got matched and won!

Do what you feel comfortable with!

Bonus Large Price Betfair Trading Strategy

I will now explain the bonus large price Betfair horse racing trading strategy and this can run in parallel with the main trading strategy outlined in this book, there will be no conflict of interest.

This works identically to the main Betfair trading strategy in this book monitoring decimal odds between 10 minutes and 10 seconds before the race starts. The difference is that we are only interested in favourites 5 to 10 (favourites 5,6,7,8,9,10) in the race.

I noticed when modelling and testing the main Betfair trading strategy in this book that certain decimal odds differential patterns repeated for favourites 5 to 10 in the betting. These decimal odds differentials were as follows,

The decimal odds differential had to be greater than or equal to 4.0 for favourites 5 to 10 in the Betfair market.

The decimal odds for favourites 5 to 10 in the Betfair market should be greater than or equal to 10.0 and less than or equal to 30.0.

These two conditions above would produce some nice profitable trades.

I will show you a couple of examples of these trades below.

27th September 2023

Goodwood 5.20 Winner Mr Professor

Decimal odds difference 10 minutes and 10 seconds before the race starts **6.0** (calculated 5 seconds before the race starts).

I actually lowered my stake from £3 to £1 as an example for this book and to show scaling back this trading strategy.

Our stake of £1 produces a profit of **£9.00**.

Decimal Odds 10 Minutes Before The Race Starts

9/27/2023 17:10:00: Arthurs Realm: Back Fav1 Price 10 Mins = 5.2
9/27/2023 17:10:00: Wind Your Neck In: Back Fav2 Price 10 Mins = 6.2
9/27/2023 17:10:00: Chips And Rice: Back Fav3 Price 10 Mins = 8.2
9/27/2023 17:10:00: Miss Bluebelle: Back Fav4 Price 10 Mins = 10
9/27/2023 17:10:00: Sly Madam: Back Fav5 Price 10 Mins = 11
9/27/2023 17:10:00: Mostawaa: Back Fav6 Price 10 Mins = 14
9/27/2023 17:10:00: Two Tempting: Back Fav7 Price 10 Mins = 16
9/27/2023 17:10:00: Mr Professor: Back Fav8 Price 10 Mins = 17
9/27/2023 17:10:00: Miss Down Under: Back Fav9 Price 10 Mins = 20
9/27/2023 17:10:00: Junkanoo: Back Fav10 Price 10 Mins = 21

Decimal Odds 10 Seconds Before The Race Starts

9/27/2023 17:19:50: Arthurs Realm: Back Fav1 Price 10 Secs = 6.2

9/27/2023 17:19:50: Wind Your Neck In: Back Fav2 Price 10 Secs = 5.9
9/27/2023 17:19:50: Chips And Rice: Back Fav3 Price 10 Secs = 10.5
9/27/2023 17:19:50: Miss Bluebelle: Back Fav4 Price 10 Secs = 13
9/27/2023 17:19:50: Sly Madam: Back Fav5 Price 10 Secs = 8.2
9/27/2023 17:19:50: Mostawaa: Back Fav6 Price 10 Secs = 16
9/27/2023 17:19:50: Two Tempting: Back Fav7 Price 10 Secs = 16
9/27/2023 17:19:50: Mr Professor: Back Fav8 Price 10 Secs = 11
9/27/2023 17:19:50: Miss Down Under: Back Fav9 Price 10 Secs = 16.5
9/27/2023 17:19:50: Junkanoo: Back Fav10 Price 10 Secs = 19.5

Decimal Odds Difference 10 Minutes And 10 Seconds Before The Race Starts

9/27/2023 17:19:55: Arthurs Realm: Diff Back Fav1 Price = 5.2 - 6.2 = -1
9/27/2023 17:19:55: Wind Your Neck In: Diff Back Fav2 Price = 6.2 - 5.9 = 0.3
9/27/2023 17:19:55: Chips And Rice: Diff Back Fav3 Price = 8.2 - 10.5 = -2.3
9/27/2023 17:19:55: Miss Bluebelle: Diff Back Fav4 Price = 10 - 13 = -3
9/27/2023 17:19:55: Sly Madam: Diff Back Fav5 Price = 11 - 8.2 = 2.8
9/27/2023 17:19:55: Mostawaa: Diff Back Fav6 Price = 14 - 16 = -2
9/27/2023 17:19:55: Two Tempting: Diff Back Fav7 Price = 16 - 16 = 0
9/27/2023 17:19:55: Mr Professor: Diff Back Fav8 Price = 17 - 11 = 6
9/27/2023 17:19:55: Miss Down Under: Diff Back Fav9 Price = 20 - 16.5 = 3.5
9/27/2023 17:19:55: Junkanoo: Diff Back Fav10 Price = 21 - 19.5 = 1.5

Decimal Odds Difference is 17.0 – 11 = 6

Our horse Mr Professor won the race 9/1.

I got decimal odds of **10.00** for a profit of **£9.00** for a **£1** stake.

26th September 2023

Lingfield 3.35 Winner Shoot To Kill

Decimal odds difference 10 minutes and 10 seconds before the race starts **8.0** (calculated 5 seconds before the race starts).

I actually lowered my stake from £3 to £1 as an example for this book and to show scaling back this trading strategy.

Our stake of £1 produces a profit of **£12.0**.

Decimal Odds 10 Minutes Before The Race Starts

9/26/2023 15:25:00: Belo Horizonte: Back Fav1 Price 10 Mins = 4.6
9/26/2023 15:25:00: Dream Of Mischief: Back Fav2 Price 10 Mins = 6
9/26/2023 15:25:00: Supaspecialawesome: Back Fav3 Price 10 Mins = 6.8
9/26/2023 15:25:00: Flying Spirit: Back Fav4 Price 10 Mins = 10.5
9/26/2023 15:25:00: Lordsbridge Girl: Back Fav5 Price 10 Mins = 10.5
9/26/2023 15:25:00: Hiromichi: Back Fav6 Price 10 Mins = 12.5
9/26/2023 15:25:00: Sonemos: Back Fav7 Price 10 Mins = 15
9/26/2023 15:25:00: Shoot To Kill: Back Fav8 Price 10 Mins = 23
9/26/2023 15:25:00: Yellow Lion: Back Fav9 Price 10 Mins = 27
9/26/2023 15:25:00: Renesmee: Back Fav10 Price 10 Mins = 36

Decimal Odds 10 Seconds Before The Race Starts

9/26/2023 15:34:50: Belo Horizonte: Back Fav1 Price 10 Secs = 6
9/26/2023 15:34:50: Dream Of Mischief: Back Fav2 Price 10 Secs = 5.1
9/26/2023 15:34:50: Supaspecialawesome: Back Fav3 Price 10 Secs = 7
9/26/2023 15:34:50: Flying Spirit: Back Fav4 Price 10 Secs = 9.4
9/26/2023 15:34:50: Lordsbridge Girl: Back Fav5 Price 10 Secs = 10.5
9/26/2023 15:34:50: Hiromichi: Back Fav6 Price 10 Secs = 12
9/26/2023 15:34:50: Sonemos: Back Fav7 Price 10 Secs = 17
9/26/2023 15:34:50: Shoot To Kill: Back Fav8 Price 10 Secs = 15
9/26/2023 15:34:50: Yellow Lion: Back Fav9 Price 10 Secs = 21
9/26/2023 15:34:50: Renesmee: Back Fav10 Price 10 Secs = 50

Decimal Odds Difference 10 Minutes And 10 Seconds Before The Race Starts

9/26/2023 15:34:55: Belo Horizonte: Diff Back Fav1 Price = 4.6 - 6 = -1.4
9/26/2023 15:34:55: Dream Of Mischief: Diff Back Fav2 Price = 6 - 5.1 = 0.9
9/26/2023 15:34:55: Supaspecialawesome: Diff Back Fav3 Price = 6.8 - 7 = -0.2
9/26/2023 15:34:55: Flying Spirit: Diff Back Fav4 Price = 10.5 - 9.4 = 1.1
9/26/2023 15:34:55: Lordsbridge Girl: Diff Back Fav5 Price = 10.5 - 10.5 = 0
9/26/2023 15:34:55: Hiromichi: Diff Back Fav6 Price = 12.5 - 12 = 0.5
9/26/2023 15:34:55: Sonemos: Diff Back Fav7 Price = 15 - 17 = -2
9/26/2023 15:34:55: Shoot To Kill: Diff Back Fav8 Price = 23 - 15 = 8
9/26/2023 15:34:55: Yellow Lion: Diff Back Fav9 Price = 27 - 21 = 6
9/26/2023 15:34:55: Renesmee: Diff Back Fav10 Price = 36 - 50 = -14

Decimal Odds Difference is 23.0 – 15 = 8

Our horse Shoot To Kill won the race 12/1.

I got decimal odds of **13.00** for a profit of **£12.00** for a **£1** stake.

3rd October 2023   100/1 In-Play!

Southwell 4.40 Winner She's A Rocca

This is a great example of a selection pinpointed by this Betfair trading strategy that hit decimal odds **100.0** in-play.

Decimal odds difference 10 minutes and 10 seconds before the race starts **5.0** (calculated 5 seconds before the race starts).

I actually lowered my stake from £3 to £1 as an example for this book and to show scaling back this trading strategy.

Initial trade our stake of £1 produces a profit of **£10.00**.

Second trade our stake of £1 produces a profit of **£99** on the second trade at decimal odds 100.0.

Decimal Odds 10 Minutes Before The Race Starts

10/3/2023 16:30:00: Heross Du Seuil: Back Fav1 Price 20 Mins = 2.44
10/3/2023 16:30:00: Redbridge Rambler: Back Fav2 Price 20 Mins = 5.2
10/3/2023 16:30:00: Roll With It: Back Fav3 Price 20 Mins = 6
10/3/2023 16:30:00: Could Be Trouble: Back Fav4 Price 20 Mins = 9
10/3/2023 16:30:00: Baileys Derbyday: Back Fav5 Price 20 Mins = 14.5
10/3/2023 16:30:00: Shes A Rocca: Back Fav6 Price 20 Mins = 16

Decimal Odds 10 Seconds Before The Race Starts

10/3/2023 16:39:50: Heross Du Seuil: Back Fav1 Price 10 Secs = 2.66
10/3/2023 16:39:50: Redbridge Rambler: Back Fav2 Price 10 Secs = 5
10/3/2023 16:39:50: Roll With It: Back Fav3 Price 10 Secs = 6.2
10/3/2023 16:39:50: Could Be Trouble: Back Fav4 Price 10 Secs = 6.4
10/3/2023 16:39:50: Baileys Derbyday: Back Fav5 Price 10 Secs = 34
10/3/2023 16:39:50: Shes A Rocca: Back Fav6 Price 10 Secs = 11

Decimal Odds Difference 10 Minutes And 10 Seconds Before The Race Starts

10/3/2023 16:39:55: Heross Du Seuil: Diff Back Fav1 Price = 2.44 - 2.66 = -0.22
10/3/2023 16:39:55: Redbridge Rambler: Diff Back Fav2 Price = 5.2 - 5 = 0.2
10/3/2023 16:39:55: Roll With It: Diff Back Fav3 Price = 6 - 6.2 = -0.2
10/3/2023 16:39:55: Could Be Trouble: Diff Back Fav4 Price = 9 - 6.4 = 2.6
10/3/2023 16:39:55: Baileys Derbyday: Diff Back Fav5 Price = 14.5 - 34 = -19.5
10/3/2023 16:39:55: Shes A Rocca: Diff Back Fav6 Price = 16 - 11 = 5

Automation in-play log extract

10/3/2023 16:41:16: Shes A Rocca: Hit 11.0 = 1
10/3/2023 16:41:16: Shes A Rocca: Hit 10.0 = 1
10/3/2023 16:41:16: Shes A Rocca: Hit 9.5 = 1
10/3/2023 16:41:16: Shes A Rocca: Hit 9.0 = 1
10/3/2023 16:41:16: Shes A Rocca: Hit 8.5 = 1
10/3/2023 16:41:16: Shes A Rocca: Hit 8.0 = 1
10/3/2023 16:41:16: Shes A Rocca: Hit 7.0 = 1
10/3/2023 16:41:16: Shes A Rocca: Hit 5.5 = 1
10/3/2023 16:41:16: Shes A Rocca: Hit 5.0 = 1
10/3/2023 16:41:16: Shes A Rocca: Hit 4.75 = 1
10/3/2023 16:41:28: Shes A Rocca: Hit 13.0 = 1
10/3/2023 16:41:28: Shes A Rocca: Hit 12.0 = 1
10/3/2023 16:45:49: Shes A Rocca: Hit 4.5 = 1
10/3/2023 16:45:57: Shes A Rocca: Hit 14.0 = 1
10/3/2023 16:45:57: Shes A Rocca: Hit 15.0 = 1
10/3/2023 16:45:59: Shes A Rocca: Hit 25.0 = 1
10/3/2023 16:46:00: Shes A Rocca: Hit 30.0 = 1
10/3/2023 16:46:00: Shes A Rocca: Hit 40.0 = 1
10/3/2023 16:46:04: Shes A Rocca: Hit 70.0 = 1
10/3/2023 16:46:04: Shes A Rocca: Hit 50.0 = 1
10/3/2023 16:46:12: Shes A Rocca: Hit 80.0 = 1
10/3/2023 16:46:13: Shes A Rocca: Hit 100.0 = 1
10/3/2023 16:46:13: Shes A Rocca: Hit 90.0 = 1
10/3/2023 16:46:19: Shes A Rocca: Hit 4.0 = 1
10/3/2023 16:46:19: Shes A Rocca: Hit 3.75 = 1
10/3/2023 16:46:19: Shes A Rocca: Hit 3.5 = 1
10/3/2023 16:46:19: Shes A Rocca: Hit 3.0 = 1
10/3/2023 16:46:23: Shes A Rocca: Hit 2.5 = 1
10/3/2023 16:46:23: Shes A Rocca: Hit 2.0 = 1
10/3/2023 16:46:23: Shes A Rocca: Hit 1.91 = 1
10/3/2023 16:46:23: Shes A Rocca: Hit 1.81 = 1
10/3/2023 16:46:23: Shes A Rocca: Hit 1.71 = 1

10/3/2023 16:46:24: Shes A Rocca: Hit 1.61 = 1
10/3/2023 16:46:25: Shes A Rocca: Hit 1.51 = 1
10/3/2023 16:46:25: Shes A Rocca: Hit 1.41 = 1
10/3/2023 16:46:25: Shes A Rocca: Hit 1.31 = 1
10/3/2023 16:46:26: Shes A Rocca: Hit 1.21 = 1
10/3/2023 16:46:26: Shes A Rocca: Hit 1.11 = 1
10/3/2023 16:46:43: Shes A Rocca: Winner = 1

Some Advice!

When using this large priced Betfair trading strategy you might want to consider using an offset bet on your trade. Let us look at this in more detail, you will be getting some juicy prices with this strategy but based on probability many of them will not win which is to be expected. So why not reduce the risk and place an offset bet on your trade(s).

For example we select a horse with decimal odds 10.0 to make it easy, we could place a second trade on our selection which is a lay bet at decimal odds 4.0. If our lay bet gets matched at decimal odds of 4.0 we have had a free bet/trade. Obviously deciding the decimal odds for the lay bet is up to you. You can take this further by greening up so you will win regardless of your selection not winning the race.

Scaling For A Full Time Living

Scaling for a full time living should be straight forward by increasing your trading stakes in increments this all depends on your trading bank. I have used small stakes in this book but these can produce some nice profits. Do not rush into increasing your trading stake get a feel for these Betfair trading strategies and be patient!

Automating These Betfair Trading Strategies

This is my favourite type of trading it is fully automated which I will make clearer later. You will need a Betfair exchange trading tool software like Bet Angel which is the one I love and use all the time. As I said earlier these trading strategies can be applied manually. I have been using this excellent software since 2007 and it has matured and is constantly being updated with new features. This is in my opinion the best Betfair trading tool on the market.

https://www.betangel.com/

My Automation Rules File

I use the brilliant Bet Angel trading software and I have coded automation rules files to execute my trades using these Betfair trading strategies outlined in this book. This allows me to run these trading strategies hands free on the UK and Irish horse racing markets. The great advantage of automation is that it does not make mistakes. If you interested in learning more please email me or visit my website outlined at the end of this book.

Conclusions

I hope you have enjoyed this main horse racing in-play Betfair trading strategy that will produce a small number of trades and long term consistent profits. Remember one trading strategy does not fit all markets but this is one Betfair trading strategy that will give you confidence and get you on your way. Use low stakes when using this strategy and gain confidence keeping a record of all your trades. I only use this strategy on UK and Irish horse racing using Betfair.

I have included some extra Betfair trading strategies that you can use but that is up to you. You could use small stakes with these extra Betfair trading strategies and get a feel for these.

Good luck!

Mark Horrocks

Email: vanderwheil6@gmail.com

Website: https://chevanderwheil.com/

Printed in Great Britain
by Amazon